Don't go looking....
It's Here...

Create your own simple quotes Book....

Janet Beaufond

Copyright 2019 Janet Beaufond
All rights reserved
ISBN: 978-1-0767-2893-7

Dedication

May you find all your answers within. You have got it all. Be anybody you want to be. Nothing is stopping you...

Peak Inspiration

Have you every had an idea or thought but do not know where to manifest this information. Well you have got the answer now. Put it on paper and see it grow!!!

Acknowledgments

To all my past & present teachers, ie anybody that I came across in my everyday life...

Thank you for your guidelines and patience in encouraging me in making me the person I am today...

H- OPE for ourselves takes place when we make a special

E- FFORT and

A- CKNOWLEDGE the fact that the

L- OVE we bring into our lives, gives us the

I- NSPIRATION to

N- URTURE our well being for our own spiritual

G- ROWTH

Love comes to those who want

Look for Balance always....

Create your own quotes here

We are both Teacher & Pupil

Create your own quotes here

The World is round but sometimes "The Key to Life" can appear to be square

Create your own quotes here

Your Heart always know the answer, listen to it.......

Create your own quotes here

Oh it is only a phone call yet it is so frightful because the unknown behind that call might only reveal a mere cool. So take courage. Have a go. Life is full of fun, yet who might be so low, but your kind thoughts helped them to enjoy the Sun again......

Create your own quotes here

Learn to give and and take....

This is The Art of Flexibility & Balance.....

Create your own quotes here

Follow What Is True

Create your own quotes here

"The Power of the Universe" Say this sincerely and see what happens!!!

Create your own quotes here

I have always been with you..... I will always be with you.....

Create your own quotes here

Inspiration sometime comes from

Listening and Waiting

Create your own quotes here

When you give Love give to the best of yourself and ask for nothing in return. What you give out was only really meant for you......

Create your own quotes here

Your Body knows its limits. Follow it. Sit on it......

Create your own quotes here

Fight only for what belongs to you....

Take action Now. Leave nothing for Tomorrow...

Create your own quotes here

No measurement for TIME...

Create your own quotes here

Remember what you believe in. You will create it.

Your head is full of ideas. Share it with others.

Be yourself today, so others can follow.

Nobody is left out. There is enough for all.

Acceptance in everything is the first step to Happiness and Freedom

Create your own quotes here

Always look for the best in others

Create your own quotes here

I believe that one day PAIN will be a thing of the Past....

OUCH....

Create your own quotes here

"First" born are Lucky & Bossy

"Middle" are Loving & Discipline

"Last" are Artistic & Carefree

Create your own quotes here

With Faith we have HOPE!!!

Create your own quotes here

Once you know your Intuition, have the Courage to follow it through!!!

Create your own quotes here

When you are feeling low let yourself be guided. When you are feeling high in glow share it with someone......

Create your own quotes here

We are Creativity, so go and Create

Create your own quotes here

Do Something Positive today.!!!

Create your own quotes here

Do not be A shame of who you really are!!!

Speak out - Let yourself be heard and be counted!!!

Nobody has got any right to judge another!!!

Create your own quotes here

I am Whole......but only a quarter Shinning....which way to go....Reality or Illusion....

Create your own quotes here

Ask for more there is Plenty.....

Create your own quotes here

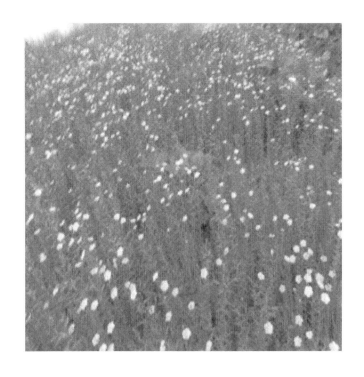

*Be not
Afraid to Stand Up to what you
Believe is Right and True*

Create your own quotes here

Remember Fear attracts only Fear, but Love and Justice attracts only Love and Justice for all.....

Create your own quotes here

Remember you can be Anything you want to be in Life......Just put it into action.... Then just see it happen before your very Eyes.....

Create your own quotes here

If anything or anyone needs to be changed, let that person be you!!!

You play into Guilt, you give the other one your Power!!!

Things move faster when we are totally Relaxed!!!

Create your own quotes here

Create your own quotes & picture here

Create your own quotes here

Remember to do your very Best and leave the Rest for the Universe

Create your own quotes here

Everybody's perception of the TRUTH is different, but the Journey is the Same

Create your own quotes here

ITS GREAT TO BE HOME -

The Inner Journey;
Is the first Discovery;
Of your True Self;
Go ahead Confidently;
In the direction it takes you.

Create your own quotes here

Communication is one of the Key to moving forward

Create your own quotes here

Reach for the Stars above within Ourselves......

Create your own quotes here

Misunderstanding among-st ourselves have created so much confusions....

Create your own quotes here

We must remember Men have Different Roles to Women. So try to change either one.....

Women or Men who loves many does not love the Woman or Man in themselves.....

Create your own quotes here

A person's BODY is priceless. So ask for none.....

Create your own quotes here

Learn to Protect your
GIFT
ENERGY
MIND
Learn to use and love your GEM well......

Create your own quotes here

Pleasing oneself sometime, is the best part of growing up

Create your own quotes here

Nobody can make you do anything you do not want to do...

SO TRUST!

Create your own quotes here

I have come a very LONG way to find you.....

Create your own quotes here

Don't go looking.... It will find you....

Create your own quotes here

There is no BEGINNING and no END

The PAST has gone

The FUTURE is yet to come

NOW is the moment

Give too much you get recent full
Give to little you become arrogant

High expectation gets you so disappointed
Low expectation makes you so very angry
So expect the very best for yourself

One small Positive thought can change a huge Core of Human Mankind

Create your own

About the Author

Janet Beaufond is a Seychelloise but was born in Kenya. She left Kenya when she was 9 years old to live in Seychelles with her father. She lived there for another 9 years when she moved to England to be with her mother. It was there that she became ill at age 36 and a big transformation took place which changed her life for ever. By going to different Therapists for healing she got to learn a lot about herself and others to the point where she took on the healing career of being a Massage Therapists. Through life's ups and down she was able to put all her experiences into this book, where she spend 3 months in solitude and with all her own words which she wrote 20 years ago. She is also a Creative Dancer and done many workshops for most of the latter part of her life. To keep herself in daily harmony she practices & teach Kundalini Yoga where she meets with like-minded people in her everyday life. She now spends most of her happy time and life with her very supportive partner in Grenada Caribbean.

Be Bothered.........

Notes

Preparation

Insight

Ideas

Finishing Touch

Made in the USA
Columbia, SC
12 September 2019